I REMEMBER WHEN DAD...

I REMEMBER WHEN DAD...

Memories and Stories about FATHERS

ARIEL BOOKS

Andrews McMeel
Publishing

Kansas City

Library of Congress Cataloging-in-Publication Data

I remember when dad . . . : memories and stories about
   fathers/collected by Louise Betts Egan.
     p. cm.
   ISBN 0-7407-3311-7
   1.Fathers. 2. Father and child. I. Betts, Louise.
HQ756.I64   2003
306.874'2—dc21

                                        2002034289

To all fathers, fathers-in-law, stepfathers, and father figures, past, present, and future.

S ay the word *father* and you might think of a man with a pipe in an armchair reading the paper. But say the words *my father* and out come a mental photo album's worth of pictures—a fleeting moment, a gesture, a laugh, an important event, a routine you did together—where Dad was at the center of the experience.

This book has gathered some of those pictures, in words, from sons and daughters of all ages and from all over the United States and the world. Here, you'll find a dad who finds time to play "beauty salon" with his young daughter, a dad who passes on the passion of his hobby to his son, and a dad who becomes driving instructor to his teenager. Dad is the one who, by example, teaches the importance of hard work yet who learns from his children how to say, "I love you."

The stories in this collection show how our fathers impress us, their children, through their kindness, strength, integrity, and humor. They may be just ordinary dads doing ordinary things, but they are unwittingly creating lasting memories and unique portraits of their humanity.

A friend once told my dad, "Travel with your children when they're young, because once they're teenagers, it's all over." Dad must have taken that to heart, because since I was very young, the two of us have done lots of traveling together—going skiing, hiking, hunting, and even white-water rafting. Dad seems to prefer doing these things one-on-one, rather than as a family with my three sisters and mom, though we've sometimes done that, too. My sisters have also gone on trips alone with him.

Those trips have been good—not only because they are great vacations, but also because I feel so comfortable around my dad. Dad works long hours when he's home. If not for those trips, I'm not sure how close I'd be with him today. I'm now out of my teens and I'd still go anywhere with him.

TREVOR, 20, WASHINGTON, D.C.

When I was ten, my dad and I went on a four-day round-trip from Rhode Island to South Africa, where Dad is from. We arrived in the morning, my aunt Alison's wedding was the next day, and we went home the day after that.

On the plane, I gave Dad one of my favorite books to read. Dad taught me a game of poker. We listened to music, ate, and slept. It was nice having my dad right next to me for so long.

I also liked seeing Dad with his family. Since they live so far away, I don't get to see them much, and it's cool to see relatives with his same mannerisms and accent!

The plane trip took seventeen hours each way, and I asked Dad if it had been worth all the traveling. He said, "Absolutely." Dad had been away from home for twelve years already and had missed so much of his little sister's life growing up. "At least I saw her get married," he said.

CAITLIN, 15, EAST GREENWICH, RHODE ISLAND

Whenever my children complain that chores are no fun, I remind them about the task my father had to do when he was young: At twelve years old, Dad had to drive his father's car across fields in the countryside so that Grandpa could shoot rabbits from the backseat. This was not for sport; it was for supper. Was it fun? Not exactly. My father remembers struggling to reach the car pedals, barely seeing over the steering wheel.

This was in the middle of the depression, before driver's licenses were necessary, before there was much traffic, and when food was not always bought in a store.

LORNA, 42, WOKING, ENGLAND

I remember first receiving letters at the age of ten, when I was at Camp Kin-ah-wee. Mom wrote faithfully, and a few younger siblings scrawled illegibly on postcards. But most of my letters came from Dad. His letters, which came several times a week, were typed on the yellow trading paper from his brokerage firm. This was the beginning of Dad's letter-writing tradition—and family legacy.

A letter from Dad came to mean home, family, and love to me and my four siblings as each of us left the nest. Dad's once-short letters became longer letters, typed on standard white paper, copied, and sent to all five of us. The letters were Dad's voice, conveying the daily-life details that no phone call ever could, and they came several times a week for about twenty years. We wrote letters home, too, normally in messy handwriting, which Dad then typed up for the rest of us and sent out. He was a father-as-scribe, connecting us to home and to each other.

FREDERICKA, 47, CHARLESTON, SOUTH CAROLINA

When I was a kid, my dad would take me down to a blues club on the south side of Chicago, where we would listen to the music and visit the owner, a friend of Dad's. Years later and in Chicago on business, I decided to visit this old haunt.

The club was still there, still in the same run-down neighborhood, and I was drawn in by the past. Inside, however, people stared at me like I did not belong. When I ordered a drink at the bar, the bartender advised me to leave once I finished it. The bartender, it turned out, was also the owner—the son of the former owner.

I told the bartender that I used to come there as a kid, and when I said Dad's name—*kaboom!*—everything changed. Suddenly, I was given the royal treatment, given drinks and dinner on the house.

Turns out, thirty-five years ago, Dad had given the owner $5,000 to stay in business and had never asked for a dime back.

WILL, 50, SANTA MONICA, CALIFORNIA

My dad is a big fan of Kiss, the seventies rock group that wears face paint and outrageous costumes. When they came to town a few years ago, Dad said, "I want your first rock concert to be memorable." So, even though I was only eight at the time, he took me to hear them. Before we went, we both painted our faces silvery white with a black star around one of our eyes, like Paul, the Kiss guitarist.

When we got to the concert, the opening act was Ted Nugent, who played so loudly, Dad and I had to leave the arena and wait by the food stands. But when Kiss came onstage, with fireworks, it was really cool. Everyone was standing up, shouting along with the music (including Dad). It was completely awesome.

As we walked out, I noticed lots of people with their faces painted, but as far as I could see, Dad and I were the only father-son pair there.

WILL, 12, DES MOINES, IOWA

I have an extremely vivid memory of walking along the beach with my father one afternoon (I was six or seven years old), waves cooling our feet every couple of steps. I was paying attention to nothing in particular, when my father abruptly planted his right foot in the sand between the ocean and me. Then—*bang!*—a four-foot plank of driftwood slammed into my father's ankle, then flipped up on edge against his leg by the force of the wave, then, slowly, got dragged back into the surf.

My father looked down at me and asked, "Are you all right?" I remember feeling a tremendous sense of awe for my father—that he would put himself in harm's way for me. I knew, then, I would always be safe with him.

DAVID, 38, SAINT LOUIS, MISSOURI

My father was born in Berlin and fought for Germany in World War I. Afterward, he returned to Berlin to operate his restaurant, settle down, and get married. He went to the local matchmaker, who said she had the perfect girl for him—a well-educated, multilingual young woman, who lived in Lithuania. Off he went to meet her and her family.

While sight-seeing there with his future brother-in-law, Dad was approached by a Russian-speaking man. He asked if Dad had been a guard at a POW camp during the war. Reluctantly—because Germans were notorious for hating Russians—Dad admitted that he had been.

The stranger excitedly shouted that he remembered my father as one German who was always kind to him and to the other prisoners. Dad had even given them cigarettes and food—in those circumstances, a remarkable display of kindness. This quality of Dad's would reverberate a generation later, with my sister—but that's another story.

HARRY, 78, MOUNT VERNON, NEW YORK

Dad's innate kindness was ultimately rewarded with a miracle:

My sister, Charlotte, was a prisoner at Stutthof, a Polish death camp during World War II. One day, while her group was working in the fields, the guard asked if any of them were from Berlin. My sister said she was and told the guard her name. It turned out that not only did the guard know our father and the restaurant, but he and Dad were good friends.

Some weeks later, the same guard escorted Charlotte's group from the field, but rather than take them back to the barracks, he locked them in a shed and said he'd return shortly. The guard knew that any inmates found in the barracks would be shipped to the crematorium. He saved Charlotte's life!

Out of 33,000 Jews in the Riga Ghetto—a place created by the Nazis and where Charlotte was forced to live before the war—only 300 survived, and just 100 were women. I credit the miracle of her survival to Dad's goodness.

HARRY, 78, MOUNT VERNON, NEW YORK

When Dad learned that he had cancer, he started building a pool in his backyard. It seemed crazy, but Dad had *big* designs for this pool: There were dancing, colored fountains, underwater speakers, and a bazillion-degree Jacuzzi (think the front lobby of Caesars Palace). Every time it seemed the pool was finally going to be finished, Dad would think of something else to add. I think he felt as long as the pool was still not finished, he couldn't die.

ELLEN, 35, COLUMBUS, GEORGIA

Words from Dad: Never start trouble with anyone, but if someone starts trouble with you, finish it.

PEGGY, 58, MONTCLAIR, NEW JERSEY

My dad took the commuter train to work every day and enjoyed his walk to the station. He liked seeing the neighborhood kids riding their bikes to school and especially loved the occasional shouted greeting, "Hi, Mr. Betts!" To get to the station, he had to walk through a park, which had an unusual water fountain set within a large rock. Dad always stopped to take a sip from this fountain.

Like other kids, I rode my bike to school and sometimes got to the park just as he was stopping for a sip of water. Whenever that happened, I'd get off my bike and take a sip of water, too. I remember the smell of his cologne as we gave each other a quick extra hug, before heading off on our separate ways.

CHARLOTTE, 28, MUSKOGEE, OKLAHOMA

When I was in Cub Scouts, one of the bigger annual events was the Pine Wood Derby. Each of us was given a little block of wood, and the rest was up to us to shape, paint, and accessorize the race car of our dreams.

One weekend afternoon, my father took me to my great-uncle Tom's house, where he had a wood shop. With Uncle Tom's son, Tommy, also on hand, the four of us drew out the shape of the car, sleek and elegant. My dad and Tommy guided my young hands on the jigsaw to carve out the shape. After that, we sanded the edges smooth and painted it a glossy black; once the car was dry, we applied some racing decals and attached the wheels. We were set!

Come race day, trial after trial, my car beat the rest. Dad and I savored our victories, until we finally won the tournament. Just as sweet as winning, I think, was the teamwork building my dream race car.

THOMAS, 29, MILFORD, CONNECTICUT

I remember when Dad started his tradition of including two lottery tickets in my birthday card. One represented my age and one had the numbers for the year I was born. Even now that I am grown up, both my husband and I still delight in this tradition. Though I have only won once in all that time, it's always good to know that I have those lottery tickets to look forward to on every birthday!

TRACEE, 27, MOUNT JOY, PENNSYLVANIA

The first time Dad met Mum, he wrote her off as too "landed gentry," or preppy. On that damp, cool spring evening in England a zillion years ago, when they were teenagers at a party held in an open garage, Mum was looking classically British, as Dad recalls, in her cable-knit fisherman's sweater, Wellington boots, and hair in a neat ponytail. Dad is naturally shy and reserved, and writing Mum off that way made sense to him at the time. Besides, Mum was dating a friend of his.

Fortunately, Dad continued to run into Mum through their mutual friends over the next few years. Slowly, Dad realized he came out of his shell around her—they laughed a lot together and became good friends while slowly falling in love.

By the time they got married, Dad's younger brother and Mum's younger sister had begun dating, and eventually married as well. And we're all living happily ever after.

HARRIET, 18, LARCHMONT, NEW YORK

My dad worked long days and didn't arrive home until seven every night, six days a week. He owned an electronics store in the Bronx and we lived in the suburb of Rockland County.

I remember getting so excited when I heard the garage door. It not only meant Dad was home (and that we could eat dinner), but we could also do one of my favorite things, a "go-round." This meant that Dad and I would hold hands and walk around the property examining all the trees, shrubs, and new bushes and plants, as well as eat the strawberries that were growing in the garden. This was our special time together and it always made me feel close to him.

I now have my own big backyard with beautiful plantings and gardens, and I hold my kids' hands and say, "Let's do a go-round." And when my dad stops by, we still do a go-round together.

RISA, 40, NANUET, NEW YORK

I remember being on vacation in Jamaica (my mom and stepfather are Jamaican), visiting a friend who owned a beautiful house and, to protect it, had six big dogs that were trained to attack.

Dave, my stepfather, and I were in the driveway, eating mangoes by our rental car. One of the dogs came out of the yard toward us, then another. "Oh my God, it's the dogs," we said, both panicking at the sight of them. Mind you, they weren't riled up or anything. On the contrary, they were just walking around, but as I said, we panicked. *Guard dogs. They were going to get us. We had to escape!* We tried to open the car doors, but with our hands slippery from the mangoes, we couldn't get into it and so scrambled onto the car roof to escape the "mad" dogs.

Once we got there, we realized how funny the situation was—two stooges on top of a car running away from nothing—and laughed until we cried.

JASMINE, 21, SIOUX FALLS, SOUTH DAKOTA

When my grandmother was very ill, my mother went to see her at a sanatorium in Michigan. I was about twenty-one and working in Chicago. I stayed with my father, who was always so special. He was in the advertising business and every time we walked across the Chicago River Bridge on Michigan Avenue, I felt like everyone on the bridge knew him—they'd all say, "Hi, Jeff!" We went to the Key Club for dinner one night while Mother was still away, and he told people that I was his girlfriend instead of his daughter, which was so funny.

GINNY, 68, LAKE FOREST, ILLINOIS

On to La Plata!" That is what Dad would say every December as we began the drive from Boston to Fort Lauderdale, where we spent every Christmas with my grandparents. It was a three-day drive down Route 1, and our first stop was the Howard Johnson's motel in La Plata, Maryland.

Before each trip, Dad would go to a magic store in Boston and buy about fifty little toys, games, or tricks. Whenever my older brother and sister and I would get too noisy in the backseat, Dad would reach into his bag and throw some toys back to us. We also stopped at the occasional souvenir stand along the way. I still love all that kind of stuff and buy it for my own kids—and for myself.

And whenever we take a long trip, no matter which direction we're headed, I always find myself saying, "On to La Plata!"

BERT, 40, AUSTIN, TEXAS

Papa and I emigrated from a small town in Mexico when I was a teenager. It was hard without Mama. Papa's strict rules, especially with dating, made life really tough for me. I know he thought he was doing his job, and that if we were still in Mexico, I'd have chaperones on my dates—but he could never see that things were different here.

After high school, I left home to be a live-in nanny and went to community college part-time. Papa didn't like it, especially when I started dating a guy he didn't like. But Papa agreed (reluctantly) that it was my life. However, when I told him I was pregnant with my boyfriend's baby, and that we had broken up, Papa was very angry. We argued a lot during my difficult pregnancy.

In the end, though, it was Papa who found me a crib, who was there at the hospital, who took care of me after the baby was born, and who is the best grandfather a new mother and baby could have.

CARI, 22, WASHINGTON, D.C.

My dad, normally mild mannered, once turned from Clark Kent into Superman. I was about nine, hanging with friends outside a laundry, where stuffed duffel bags were piled into a panel truck. Each of us took a turn getting tied up and hidden within the truck. When it was my turn inside the truck, suddenly the driver appeared. No one said anything, and he didn't see me. So he slammed the door shut and took off. My best friend ran alongside the truck. When it passed my parents' luncheonette, he ran in and said, "Henry's in the truck!"

Dad, fearing I'd been kidnapped, leaped over the counter, raced out of the luncheonette, jumped onto the running board of the moving vehicle, and while he was trying to take the wheel through the driver's open window, bellowed, "Stop the truck!"

My friend quickly explained what had happened. The driver, shaken, opened the back door and there I was. Superman quickly became Clark Kent again, too relieved to be mad.

HENRY, 64, NEW YORK, NEW YORK

When I was quite young, my father would tell me stories about a little orange trolley car that came complete with illustrations, drawn on the spot, of the LOTC's adventures. I wish we had kept those pictures and somehow recorded the stories. Maybe they would only be special from your own dad, but I know I enjoyed them. My mom made me a handkerchief with the LOTC drawn on it, but I've lost that, too.

My dad is a rail fan, someone who finds certain aspects of railroading intriguing, and he has passed that interest on to me. So it was no surprise that when a railroad-oriented museum was founded in our town, he was one of the founders. I got involved later on and eventually became the museum's president. Dad is the chief engineer, as in civil engineer, of his profession. The centerpiece of this museum is a little trolley car, painted . . . yellow. You didn't really think things worked out *that* simply, did you?

ROBERT, 40, SHELBURNE FALLS, MASSACHUSETTS

When Dad was courting Mom, he was stationed at an army base not far from her home in Oklahoma. Dad was a young man from Chicago, a city boy, who couldn't tell a Guernsey cow from a Jersey—a serious character flaw to Grandpa, who was not at all convinced that Dad was "the one" for his daughter.

It was during this courting time that Grandpa lent Dad his car so he and Mom could go out on a date. On the way home, Dad accidentally hit a cow, which bent the bumper. Dad lurched to a halt, leaped out of the car, adrenaline pumping, and smoothed out the bumper with his bare hands. Dad was sure if the bump had been detected, he never would have gotten to marry Mom.

Actually, Mom said that when Grandpa eventually found out, he said, "The heck with the car—what happened to the cow?" (She lived.)

JOHN, 45, KANSAS CITY, MISSOURI

MY FATHER'S STORIES

had impossible rhythms

wads of words

attached to them.

(His soul knew no brevity.)

There were the tangled lines

of the ships he had sailed

and the Saint Bernard

he rode as a kid

on the streets of his Irish Boston.

On the one hand

he was desperate:

the million dollars

he swore he could earn.

On the other: the tattered

Brooks Brothers suit

sprayed with constant whiskey.

Belligerent in his disdain,

skidding on ice

smashing family cars

knocking down
our pathetic tree
(to say nothing
of the chief of police).
And yet, there were

the sudden acts
of generosity,
and the tears of laughter
as he told
his preposterous tales

of India and China,
the Chelsea Hotel.
Tears running down his face
and mine.

BRIGID, 52, NEW YORK, NEW YORK

My dad, a native German, came to America at the end of World War II with nothing but optimism and a desire to work. He had heard that America's sidewalks were paved with gold and that if you simply bent over, you could pick it up.

Dad met and married my mother, also a German immigrant, here. His first job was as a milkman. After sacrificing and saving, and with the fifth child on the way, Dad opened a cabinetmaking shop in a rented garage. He worked relentlessly and without complaint to give us all the things we needed.

As teens, my brother and I spent so many hours working with Dad, my mother said, a little enviously, that we spent more time with her husband than she did. (If only I'd appreciated that then, but what teenager does?) To this day, my dad firmly believes that the golden pavements of America do exist, and that with just a little elbow grease, this country has supplied everything his family has needed.

MATTIAS, 41, CINCINNATI, OHIO

Dad was as large and jolly as Jackie Gleason, and he sported clothes as flashy as Elvis Presley's—shiny, multipatterned shirts with gold necklaces and big rings on his chubby fingers. Dad's high spirits were infectious and he had a million friends. Still, I realized when I was about nine years old that I was probably more mature than he was.

Dad would take us "skating" in his truck on frozen lakes. We slipped and slid over the ice, with Dad as raucous as a cowboy. He would cheat ticket takers for rides at amusement parks—just for fun. Dad's cars (mainly Mercedes) were regularly stolen because he'd leave the keys in and motor running while he went to do something. He never understood there were consequences for his actions.

Once I implied that he was not down-to-earth. "What?!" he exclaimed, offended. "I'm as down-to-earth as you can get!" To which I replied, "Dad, the only thing holding you even remotely close to this earth is the weight of your gold jewelry!"

LISA, 36, BOULDER, COLORADO

My dad once spent six months hand-polishing a concave piece of glass with a silk rag, for a telescope he was making. Finally, it was done, but as he headed down the stairs from the attic, he tripped! The glass broke and Dad was devastated. What a nutty genius he is!

SLIM, 30, BURLINGTON, VERMONT

My dad, born and raised in New Jersey, was the son of Irish parents. Although Dad grew up never seeing Ireland and always looking toward New York City, he longed to march in the Saint Patrick's Day Parade, but he never could. Later, he went west to college and then spent decades in the Far East for work, before finally settling in California. But he never forgot about walking in the Saint Patrick's Day Parade.

Two years ago, timed with his and Mom's golden anniversary, Dad, with Mom at his side, gathered together his three brothers and their families, and us four sons and our families. We were an enormous clan, bundled up in hats and jackets as we set off in the cold, blustery wind and rain. All together, and smack in the middle of the enormous parade, we walked from Forty-fourth Street, past Saint Patrick's Cathedral, and up Fifth Avenue to Eighty-sixth Street, for the exuberant march of a lifetime.

BRENDAN, 49, KING OF PRUSSIA, PENNSYLVANIA

My father was diagnosed with kidney failure in 1967, when kidney transplants were only just becoming available. Dad's bad kidney was removed and transplanted with one from a woman who'd been in a fatal accident. Still, Dad had to fight mind, body, and spirit to keep from rejecting it.

Turns out Dad was a model transplant. He even allowed experimental drugs to be tested on him: The doctors saw that he had the will and strength to endure any side effects. And in that way, Dad helped pave the way for progress.

Dad—who joked that now that he had a woman's kidney, he had to sit down to pee—lived another dozen years, an astonishing record back then. During that time, he toured the hospital regularly to bolster the spirits and determination of those in similar predicaments.

In his obituary, Dad was praised for his ability to encourage and instill hope in others; the enormous good that he did helps me see a purpose behind the disease that shortened his life.

JIM, 51, NORTH SCITUATE, RHODE ISLAND

Dad was a kind, gentle man who adored my mom. He was a watch salesman and didn't have a regular office, since he drove to different stores around the city and outlying areas.

When he and Mom first met, Mom was working in an office that looked out onto their hometown's main street. Whenever Dad was in the area, he'd park his car and go over to the sidewalk across from the window to Mom's office. Her desk was near the window and he'd call to her, wave exuberantly, or just wait until she looked out and saw him. Mom loved it—and has shown us the window and told us that story so many times, it was the first anecdote that came to mind.

GEORGE, 55, WHITE RIVER JUNCTION, VERMONT

Daddy loved his dogs. We had four, sometimes five, dogs at all times—retrievers, terriers, Irish bloodhounds, basset hounds, dachshunds—you name it. And although he had four children, we took the backseat when it came to getting fed at mealtime. Instead, Dad would feed the dogs first as they hovered near his chair at the head of the table. He'd stand carving the meat and making sure each dog got a sufficient share. As the dogs smacked away or whimpered for more, my stomach grumbled. But feeding the dogs was very important to him, and because we loved Dad, we just accepted it.

You may be sure, however, that no dog of mine ever got fed anything but dog food, and only in the kitchen!

JANE, 74, OKLAHOMA CITY, OKLAHOMA

ometimes I wake up on a Sunday morning, my room-
mate gone and the dorm quiet. With my eyes closed,
and being half asleep, I'll occasionally think I'm back at home
and that Dad's about to go out for his weekend breakfast. If I
get up soon, I'll be able to join him. He always likes to go out
for breakfast on the weekends and is happy whenever any of
us kids want to go with him. I'm psyched for a bagel and
scrambled eggs at our favorite diner.

Then I open my eyes—and realize I'm far away from
home, that there's a cafeteria downstairs where my meal ticket
will get me my Sunday breakfast. But rolling over and imagin-
ing a breakfast with Dad seems like a much better idea.

CONNIE, 19, EUGENE, OREGON

One time, when I was married and giving a dinner party, the cook looked out the kitchen window and asked, "Who is that man coming to your party?" I told her he was my father. The cook said she had seen him at the grocery store earlier that day, when she'd had her hair in curlers. He'd said, "Trick or treat," as he thought it was terrible to go out that way. Then, when the cook had gone to another store later that same day, and out of her curlers, my father happened to be there, too. When he saw her, he said, "Now, don't you feel proud of yourself for looking so nice?"

LAURA, 60, BILLINGS, MONTANA

My father escaped Nazi Germany in the 1930s and spoke with a thick German accent. His education was interrupted and he became an Israeli construction worker instead of the engineer he dreamed of being.

After twenty years in Israel, he began corresponding with an American pen pal, who, shortly after they met, became his wife. The two became parents to two girls, with a new life in Florida. Dad loved Beethoven, valued education, and loved simple things—like having his little girls run to his pickup truck after a day's work.

Dad loved America because he knew what life was like without freedom. He always voted with his daughters in tow.

He scrimped and saved to send his children to the state university. His car proudly bore the bumper sticker "My daughter graduated from UF Law School" and was equally proud that his other daughter became a successful businesswoman.

He believed hard work and education were the tickets to everything. He was right.

MIRA, 42, NEW YORK, NEW YORK

Dad is from Massachusetts and partial to the dry, understated humor of New England. I grew up on that humor, thrived on it. There was a time when Dad would tell us a continuing story at dinner about three men named Myrus, Fyrus, and Gyrus, who were floating down a river on a marble slab that had a magic trapdoor. Whenever disaster was upon them, one of the guys would open up the trapdoor and get just the thing to save them—a six-pack of beer, or a mind's eye (to see things in, of course).

Any interruption meant the end of the story for that night, and the story would not continue until we could remind Dad what had happened the time before. One night, none of us could remember, and the story just sort of faded away.

The adventures are lost to our fuzzy memories, but Dad and his sense of humor continue to color our lives.

SAM, 44, LEYDEN, MASSACHUSETTS

I grew up on a farm in England with a father who was rather short on words. So it was surprising when, one summer, Dad showed his family—and our whole village—a secret talent he had.

When I was about ten, the circus came to town. My sister and I were thrilled to be going with our parents, and to our amazement, Dad volunteered to be in one of the acts.

A man led a white stallion into the ring, and we watched, astonished, as Dad proceeded to ride barefoot and standing up on the horse's back as it galloped around the ring, and Dad perfectly at ease. (Apparently, this dismayed the circus folk, who were trying to show how hard this feat was.) We laughed and cheered, amazed and proud.

DIANA, 45, LOUISVILLE, KENTUCKY

D ad was born and raised in Ohio and lived on farms his first twenty-nine years. After marrying Mom in 1917, he moved his family to Phoenix, Arizona, where the summer temperature gets up to around 120 degrees. But Dad never seemed aware of that.

At six foot one and 145 pounds, Dad was all muscle and bones and had a seemingly permanent chill: He wore a button-down shirt and a suit coat the year round. If the temperature got below sixty degrees, Dad pulled the collar of his overcoat up around his neck and held it with his hand. He wore a hat, too, of course—a proper brimmed felt hat for most of the year; a straw hat as his nod to summer. Otherwise, he even drove his car with the windows rolled up, no air conditioner—a moving sauna bath.

Dad said he'd promised himself in Ohio that when he got money ahead, he'd move to where it was always warm. And he still intended to do that.

DALE, 72, LA HABRA, CALIFORNIA

Two years ago, Dad was with me when I got my driver's license. This was a big moment, one that I'd been looking forward to since Dad first put me on a merry-go-round. I've always loved cars and anything that moved. Dad was also with me for my first bumper car ride and first go-kart adventure. For my fourth, sixth, and tenth birthdays, he gave me remote control cars, each one a little fancier than the last. I still have them, though they stopped working years ago.

As I drove Dad and myself home from the Department of Motor Vehicles that day, Dad said he was proud of me. I remember thinking how cool it was to be the driver, with Dad in the passenger seat. At the moment, I didn't think to thank him for his guidance, calm instruction, and hours spent with me in the car, as I practiced. Just in case I forgot, here's another thanks. And, Dad, are you using your car tonight?

JEREMY, 17, KENNEWICK, WASHINGTON

I remember when Dad and I took a trip together to Clayton, New York, to visit Grandpa—an eight-hour drive through farm country, and no radio from Poughkeepsie onward. But we shared musical preferences and had selected cassettes.

An hour or two north, Dad switched off the static and groped for the cassette box, but it wasn't there—accidentally left behind. We gawked at the lone REO Speedwagon tape popping out like a tongue from the dashboard's mouth. Jovially, we endured, dog howling along with the lingering *R*s the lead singer imposed and reimposed upon us. To this day, we still laugh about this, *togetherrrrrr!*

REBECCA, 34, BUXEROLLES, FRANCE

My dad is a rock musician, playing in a band (not famous) that is sometimes gone for months at a time. My friends always think it's cool when I tell them what my dad does for a living. But it has also meant that he hasn't been there for big chunks of my life.

I thought I wanted to be a rock musician, too, when I grew up. I don't know why—I guess it seemed like fun. When Dad is home and just playing locally, we get to go hear the band play. Dad has also helped me learn electric guitar—and with Dad on drums, our sessions can really crank!

But when Dad was on the road in Australia when I graduated from high school, it changed my mind about what I wanted to do with my life (that, and the fact that I stink at guitar). Music will always be a part of it, but I never want a job that takes me away from my family for such a long time.

ZACHARY, 20, CLIFFSIDE PARK, NEW JERSEY

Just days before his wedding, Dad broke both legs playing basketball and went down the aisle in a wheelchair, his legs like two white torpedoes. Mom should have fled right then. But Mom was a naive eighteen-year-old from the Bronx who was attracted to Dad's larger-than-life personality and his offer of a better, and certainly different, life upstate.

My brother and I were products of that turbulent ten-year union. Dad then married our baby-sitter and had three more kids. One of those was a boy he named Stephen, after him-self—something *just not done* in our Jewish tradition. Wife number three, a neighbor, also had a son named Stephen, so suddenly there were three Stephens under one roof!

Dad did not hear the word *no,* not even with Christmas, which we didn't celebrate. Dad always brought out his beloved silver Christmas tree with blue balls, its metallic skirt, and kaleidoscopic effect. He shopped for presents and wrapped them, happy as a kid in a candy shop.

ELYSE, 37, NEW ROCHELLE, NEW YORK

We had just moved to the French part of Switzerland. All of us could speak French except Dad, who just mangled any words he tried to say. It happened that a friend of a friend of my dad's needed a place to stay for a while, and she offered to teach Dad the language.

Mademoiselle B. was very nice, but, being a bit on the chubby side, was rather obsessed with her weight. Without knowing it at the time, she and Dad became the perfect pair.

Dad could never just sit and be taught. Rather, since he worked from home, he simply had Mademoiselle follow him on his errands: He always jogged to town, then walked briskly once there. All this in the summer heat.

After just a few weeks, Dad had actually learned some French, and Mademoiselle, who by the end of each day was practically frothing at the mouth from physical exertion, had lost a good bit of weight.

MASSOUMEH, 42, GENEVA, SWITZERLAND

There may be three men in the world who don't enjoy watching or playing team sports. My dad is one of them, but I never realized that while growing up. This is a huge credit to Dad, because I was passionate about sports, still am, especially team sports, whether it was to watch or to play. Dad never let this difference come between us. In fact, he seemed to have gone out of his way to be involved with me and my sports.

When I was in grade school, Dad let me organize Sunday football games with my friends, and he was the coach. Dad was always around for playing catch and managed the games at all my baseball birthday parties. From kindergarten through twelfth grade, he watched my school games.

The one sport Dad likes is long-distance bike riding, which he usually does alone. But sometimes I'd go with him, and we were always a team, even when I was six and just mastering my two-wheeler.

IAIN, 19, INDIANAPOLIS, INDIANA

My father is a very serious and dedicated orthopedic surgeon who rarely has the chance to come home, and when he is home, he rarely gets to spend time with my two younger sisters or me. So I treasure the time we have.

When I was little, Dad and I would watch *The Little Mermaid* on video into the late hours of the night. We would fast-forward to the part where Ariel sings "Part of Your World," and at the chorus, my Dad and I would sing at the top of our lungs and dance around the room until the song was over.

Sometimes I feel like my father is detached from my life, because he is always working. But when I think back to those late nights of singing to Disney, I realize that he was trying his hardest to be "part of my world." He was, lovingly, trying to be the best dad he could be, and he most definitely is!

ELISABETH, 16, ANDOVER, MASSACHUSETTS

I was ten years old back in 1966, when an ice storm tore down the power lines and tree branches in our neighborhood. Our modern house was suddenly the equivalent of a log cabin, with central heating coming from the fireplace in our family room. We slept in sleeping bags in front of the fire, and on the first of several nights, my dad read to us from Edgar Allan Poe. Dad's demeanor, normally so mild mannered and friendly, took on the mystery of Poe's stories, his face shadowed by the flickering flames and his voice low and gravelly, as Poe would have wanted.

I will never forget Dad reading, "It is the beating of his hideous heart," the last line of that first night's story—and to this day, "The Telltale Heart" and my father are linked in one of my favorite childhood adventures.

HELEN, 46, ENID, OKLAHOMA

When I was sixteen, my father took my friend Susan and me on a late-winter camping trip on Mount Washington in New Hampshire. Up we hiked, practically straight up for four miles, carrying backpacks, sleeping bags, a cookstove, food, and skis!

We then had an incredible day of skiing, and even ice climbing, which scared us to death. In the late afternoon, as Susan and I made camp at our hut, my father surprised us by pulling a beer out of his backpack. After sharing it with us, off he went to the lodge below (as planned) for the night. The next morning, he arrived just as we were waking up and ate breakfast with us, before we set off on another great day.

That weekend showed me strengths and abilities I didn't know I had—thanks to Dad. He was hands-on when I needed him and hands-off when I didn't. Dad showed me then, and over time, the value of living with curiosity, joy, and a can-do attitude.

BLYTHE, 36, ANN ARBOR, MICHIGAN

Mom and Dad always stayed in the dining room at the table while we kids cleared the dinner dishes to make room for dessert. One night, I proudly brought out a dessert that I had made myself: Indian pudding, made with cornmeal, milk, and molasses, something our family had never had before.

While everyone else was busy scooping vanilla ice cream onto their pudding, Dad quietly excused himself, bringing his dessert bowl with him. I had never seen Dad clear his own place before, so I was a little mystified. Then I heard the *clink, clink, clink* as he scraped his pudding from the bowl into the trash. Oh, well. How typical of Dad to try to avoid offending me. Now we joke about "the time Dad cleared his dessert."

JEANNIE, 28, EVANSTON, ILLINOIS

My dad was the leader of the Cub Scouts in our town, and every year he organized a talent show for all the different troops. Dad was usually in one of the skits and one of my favorite ones was this:

A white sheet was stretched across the stage area and then lit so anything behind the sheet was a shadow. Dad then lay on a table, as if in an operating room. My friend's dad was the doctor, pretending to perform some serious surgery on Dad. He first took a saw and, after waving it up high, faked like he was opening Dad up. Then he'd appear to reach into his stomach and pull out all kinds of stuff, like an alarm clock, an extra-long flagpole that the doctor just kept pulling up and up, and a big teddy bear. All this to the shouts and laughter of a hundred young boys. Now, that was showbiz!

WHIT, 33, BIRMINGHAM, ALABAMA

When I was thirteen and newly conscious of my looks, a friend suggested that I get bangs to soften my large forehead. I took her advice—then came home and burst into tears. I hated my new look!

Seeking privacy, I went down to the basement. Dad found me, and the two of us sat on an old mattress while he related haircut horror stories of his own youth. When he was six, he even tried to kick the barber! We both got to laughing.

Then Dad found some old photographs of me when I was much younger and had bangs. I had forgotten about that time, and thought I looked kind of cute. Then Dad and I started talking about other things not related to my hair at all.

The next time I looked in the mirror, I sighed, because bangs take a long time to grow out, but then I smiled inside, because I didn't really look that bad after all.

ALICE, 15, MINNEAPOLIS, MINNESOTA

My family and I were vacationing on a lake in Canada when I was about ten years old. One day, Dad and I set out in a canoe, while my sister set out in a kayak. Mom stayed behind to rest and read.

Dad and I were having a great time—we were going fast and smoothly, which I thought was because we were so good at canoeing. Later, I realized the current and wind had been the trick. To go home, Dad tried and tried to paddle against the current. Despite his strong efforts, we were stuck. Still, Dad stayed calm, so I did, too.

Suddenly, a man on a Jet Ski appeared—with my sister on the back! She had gotten lost and flagged him down. Neither of them expected to see more of her family stranded on the lake, but there we were! Dad took the rescue in stride, graciously thanking the man for towing us all back to our cabin and much-relieved Mom.

NOAH, 13, YOUNGSTOWN, OHIO

To think of Dad and our Bethlehem house under construction brings back memories. The scent of sawdust, the banging of hammers, the suction of mud on your shoes. How else would we know about two-by-four railings, exposed beams, concrete foundations, antique fire extinguishers, and dismantling barns—and the whole process and pain of home construction!

Our beautiful home was reconstructed from a barn that Dad took apart piece by piece, painstakingly marking each beam to reassemble in a new location. Our home had custom details like stained-glass windows, doors made of original barn siding, huge fireplaces, screened porches, and solar windows that made you feel like you were part of the great outdoors. So we had to live with plywood floors for a while, so Dad forgot about closet space, so we didn't have grass for a few years. What we got in return was worth it—the experience of living in a work of art.

KERI, 31, BETHLEHEM, CONNECTICUT

In many ways, my dad was a man of his time: He never watched my mother give birth. He probably never changed a diaper or told me a bedtime story. We didn't do things "as a family" on the weekends, and he never came to my school sports events. He smoked cigarettes and sometimes had one too many cocktails. He wore a freshly laundered Brooks Brothers shirt and a suit and tie to work. And ankle garters for his socks. He tucked his newspaper under his arm as he walked to the train station. He loved my mom's cooking and always said so. He listened to his children but loved to talk. He had lots of opinions but mostly kept his personal feelings to himself. He believed in working hard and playing hard. He wore dentures, but his hair stayed blond, until after the chemo. He loved a big party. He loved being home with his family. Maybe he sounds like other dads, but to me, he was my one and only dad, and the best kind: devoted, kind, intelligent, and tremendously loving in his own way.

BETSY, 35, ALEXANDRIA, VIRGINIA

Dad was married four times before he had me, his only child (that I know of!). I guess he took his own dad's advice about never being afraid to fail ... which he did over and over, until he got it right.

MICHEL, 16, LITTLE ROCK, ARKANSAS

The night before I graduated from boarding school, my family and I were invited to my English teacher's house for a small party. In the car on the way there, I quietly announced that the movie actor Gregory Peck would be there, too, because his daughter was in my English class.

I was desperate not to be embarrassed by my family. I pleaded with them, "Please don't make fools of yourselves *and* me. And don't ask for his autograph, okay?"

Within a minute of our arrival, Dad took me aside and said, "Well, Marie, I took the bull by the horns." He showed me the back of his business card. It said, "To Dave—All the best, Greg Peck."

"Oh, Dad, you didn't!" I groaned, absolutely mortified.

Dad paused, then said, "Of course, I didn't! Look—it's my own handwriting! I just thought I'd pull your leg." Well, pull it he did, and years later, we still laugh at how he took advantage of a perfect setup.

MARIE, 44, DEERFIELD, MASSACHUSETTS

My dad and I like to stay up late and drive around our town and look at houses and observe the paint colors, because we are painting our house. My dad has taught me the names of columns and kinds of windows because of this. I really like driving with him because he likes to hear about my school day and he always has a funny story to tell about his day at work. When we're in the car, my dad teaches me jokes and what he calls "the art of humor."

EMILY, 13, MAMARONECK, NEW YORK

When I think of my dad, I think of sports: We go to professional football and baseball games; he goes to my soccer, basketball, and baseball games, and definitely comes to my karate belt matches. Sometimes we just play catch in the street or he helps me practice soccer. Those are the times we have together.

SAM, 9, LANSING, MICHIGAN

Dad's college friends nicknamed him "the King," which was short for "the King of Rock and Roll." This wasn't because he played so well—it was because he played so loud, and so often, and loved imitating different rock stars.

Dad says that Elvis Presley was the real king of rock and roll, but my friends don't know that. So, when I tell them I'm taking guitar lessons from the King of Rock and Roll, they say, "Who's that?" And I say, "My dad."

NICK, 10, PORTLAND, MAINE

My dad loves sailing, and he has managed to pass this passion on to me. This was not a given—I live in New York City, and though Dad's work often has him out at the city docks and around ships, my days are pretty landlocked, in school.

One of our early trips did not go so well either. We were on a fishing boat in Sheepshead Bay, when I got seasick. Dad tried to perk me up, without success. I felt so bad: Dad had skippered sailboats millions of times and worked on oceangoing vessels, but I couldn't make it around a bay.

Later, I overheard Dad telling Mom that he had felt seasick, too, though he hadn't said anything for fear of alarming me. I told Dad it was a big relief to know it wasn't just me, and he added that even some of the "old salts" were grumbling about the day's bad fishing—barely half a dozen caught, and, of course, none by Dad and me.

FRED, 17, NEW YORK, NEW YORK

The word *buoyant,* which means lighthearted and cheerful, has an extra meaning in our family, where it is defined as "feeling totally ridiculous," thanks to Dad. This goes back to a family vacation when we were going scuba diving. The instructor noted how Dad floated effortlessly in the water, even with all his equipment on, and called him "too buoyant." Apparently, Dad's extra body weight (though he wasn't fat) made him too light, and he needed extra metal weights added to his belt to keep him down.

Finally, we were all set and diving in the ocean wonderland. But when I looked around for Dad, I saw him on the bottom clutching a rock, his legs vertical above him as he clung to stay down. The next minute, the rock came loose and he was sent swimming helplessly upward, feet first, still holding on to the rock. It's always been a good thing that Dad could laugh at himself.

LIZ, 38, CHEYENNE, WYOMING

My father is an engineer, an exacting man, who follows instructions, and the more detailed, the better. His manner can be like that of a general: He's always right and does not know the word *sorry.* On one vacation in Europe, my mother was having difficulty opening a carton of yogurt for breakfast. As she struggled with the carton, Dad came into the kitchen and said rather insultingly, "This carton has been designed, ma'am, so that any Swiss peasant can open it up in a simple move."

Sheepishly, Mom handed the carton over for him to open "in a simple move." Hmmm. It seemed Dad was having difficulty as well but, of course, could not admit it.

After a good deal of wrestling, the carton exploded, its thick, white, liquidy mass landing on my dad's head and dripping down his face into his full black beard. We kids burst out laughing and exclaimed, "Any Swiss peasant!" Then we had Dad get down on his knees and apologize to Mom.

FARMAN, 40, VERBIER, SWITZERLAND

My parents didn't make me play team sports in elementary school, but they did have me play in the school band.

When middle school loomed and I could choose between staying with the band or dropping out, I wanted to drop out. But Dad wouldn't let me. He said, "I want you to work at something, to become good at something, and right now the only thing you can become good at is clarinet." My dad was usually a fair guy, but in this case, he gave me no choice.

I told him the band was competitive, that you had to try out to get in. He said, "If you practice hard and don't get chosen, I'll understand. But if you don't practice and don't get in, I'll be disappointed."

Band was hard and I had to practice to stay in it. I had to get to school early for practices, sometimes three or more times a week. But I did get good at it, torture that it was.

ED, 19, BROOK PARK, OHIO

My dad was a high school principal, as strict at home as he was at work, gruff and intimidating, especially to me and my siblings, who lived for his approval.

One night, when I was seventeen, Dad was driving me up to my evening job at the mall. We were quiet in the car, but I did have something urgent to ask. Finally, I blurted out: "Dad, do you love me?"

"Of course I do."

"But you've never told me that you do."

Dad then pulled the car over to the side of the highway and gave me the biggest hug. Through my tears, I could hear how choked up he was as he said, "Maureen, please never doubt that I love you more than words can say."

On this day, my dad changed forever. He started telling all of us kids how much he loved us. Twenty-five years later, Dad's still gruff, but his love is spoken often and freely and felt very deeply.

MAUREEN, 42, EAST ISLIP, NEW YORK

My dad is a night owl, staying up and working or reading or listening to music long after I've gone to bed. When I was a little girl, nothing was more comforting when waking up in the middle of the night than seeing the light coming from the living room, where Dad was doing his thing. He'd have me sit on the couch with him and I'd crawl into his lap and fall back asleep.

Cocho, 20, Forth Worth, Texas

One night we were talking about whether I would ever be bald when I grew up. Mom thinks I won't be bald, because that trait comes from the mother's side and no one on her side of the family has ever been bald. But my dad is bald, and his dad, my grampa, is, too. So, I want to be bald. I think being bald is more fatherly.

NATE, 12, LEYDEN, MASSACHUSETTS

I grew up with three sisters and no brothers. I'm sure my father wanted a son—in fact, before I was born, my parents were so sure I was a boy that they planned to name me George. But Dad never said anything about it. Instead, he taught us all "boy" things, such as woodworking and how to make slingshots. I even had my own set of Hot Wheels cars and racetracks.

Looking back, I'd say my sisters and I were lucky to have had such a rich experience. Because our father didn't distinguish between masculine and feminine activities or jobs, we didn't either. The whole world was open to us.

SUE, 40, OAKLAND, CALIFORNIA

Back in 1969, when I was thirteen years old and real men never cried, Dad took my sister, my best friend, Skip, and me to see the movie *Goodbye, Mr. Chips*. The ending was sad, and in the dim light of the theater, I saw tears—*tears*—glistening in Dad's eyes. I froze, paralyzed with fear that Skip would notice and blab this news to everyone in school. I would be mercilessly mocked.

When I suggested noisily to Skip that we get more popcorn, he seemed annoyed and told me to be quiet. The movie ended, Dad dried up, and I figured I was safe.

But in the car on the way home, my sister asked, "Dad, were you crying at the end?" And Dad (a man ahead of his time, I now realize) admitted that, yes, he was.

Skip and I exchanged glances. I figured I was doomed, but Skip actually was a good friend and never mentioned the incident to anyone.

CARL, 46, ALBERT LEA, MINNESOTA

My dad has always prided himself on being a fixer. So when my sister's brand-new watch fogged up, she went to him for advice. "Beads of water or steam can be taken out by gently heating the watch," Dad told her confidently.

After much debate over the method, my sister tried leaving the watch in the sun and when that didn't work, held a hair dryer to it—also unsuccessful. So she asked Dad to fix it.

"I'll have it back to you in no time," Dad said.

A couple hours later, my mom sniffed a strange, burning odor. Dad, who doesn't usually pay attention to culinary matters, jumped up and ran to the kitchen. He emerged with a mass of blue goop, having forgotten about the watch that he'd left in the oven.

IMMACULADA, 28, BERKELEY, CALIFORNIA

My dad is a lawyer in a three-piece suit. With a straggly ponytail. Who's otherwise bald. In college, he protested against political corruption and Watergate. He also taught swimming to handicapped children and married my mom, who was in a sorority. (Okay—a politically liberal, local one. This was the early seventies.)

As a dad, he always encouraged me to pursue my own interests, even if (or especially if) they weren't everyone else's. I play the sitar and have a pet iguana. I love to play baseball, and even though Dad doesn't, he would still come to my games all through childhood.

What I've learned from Dad is that not everyone has to fall into a certain category—sports guy, fraternity guy, nerd, or freak—that you can combine likes, dislikes, and seeming opposites to make yourself the person you want to be.

MICAH, 24, PEARL CITY, HAWAII

I was an only child. My glamorous parents loved city life and going from club to club, so our lives rarely intersected. But Dad was able to bridge the gap in our lives in a unique way—by teaching me the Gettysburg Address.

Dad began when I was about four, teaching me a few words or a sentence, which I would then memorize. I loved these private moments with him. We both felt successful, he in the teaching and me in the learning. Time passed.

When word got out in school that I could recite this, I had to perform it in front of the whole school. I was in first grade; that stage was awfully big and scary, but I did it.

I did not care for the school fame or names like "Smarty Pants," which dogged me afterward. My reward, one that made all the trouble worthwhile, was having my father be so proud of me.

BEVERLY, 67, BROOKLYN, NEW YORK

The first time I asked Dad for advice caught him off guard. I was ten years old and in a fifth-grade class with kids who were dating and having boy-girl parties on the weekend. I was not into any of that and felt bad.

I asked Dad one day, "Why am I such a loser just because I don't like any girls in my class?" Dad stalled and coughed like a car on empty. Finally, he said, "Maybe we could go to the library and find a book on this."

The library?! A book? Now I was alarmed. Dad must have thought I was a serious geek. I felt doomed and refused to go.

That night Dad came up to my room. He reminded me of all the times Jenny, from down the block, played with me—how we'd laugh and always know what to say and do. That was perfect for now, he said. The rest would follow when I was ready.

His advice has been good ever since.

BRENDON, 16, BALTIMORE, MARYLAND

My dad had a certain whistle, one he used my whole life to signal that he needed something or, as a grandfather, to announce that he was coming up the walk for a visit. It went: *DOO-de-DOO-de-DOO-DOO-DOO-DOO*. As a girl hearing that, I'd go out to the yard to see what he wanted. Later, my kids would shout out, "Gramps is here!"

One time, Dad's whistle was especially useful. My parents were on vacation in Fort Lauderdale and being run ragged by the college kids on spring break. On the phone, they sounded miserable, and I thought maybe a surprise visit would cheer them up. My daughter and I arrived at their motel a few mornings later. I knocked and called out, "Mom!" But she and Dad apparently thought I was a college kid mistaking their room for a friend's. From inside, they kept shouting, "You've got the wrong room!" Finally, I pursed my lips and gave Dad's call. It worked: I heard my mom say, "Oh, heavens, Richard—it's Dot!"

DOT, 70, LAS CRUCES, NEW MEXICO

ink-slipped. I'd never heard that odd term until it happened to my dad when I was in third grade, in 1988. Dad was upset about being laid off, and I knew that even though he suddenly had free time, it didn't feel like vacation. But his attitude was "Now my job is to find a job."

My sisters and brother and I all had ideas for his next job: a circus clown, a school custodian (the one at my school was a cool guy), a bank teller (get to touch hundred-dollar bills!), and speed car racer. We felt, and still do, that Dad would be the best guy for any job he wanted.

While Dad job-hunted, he took time out to go on a class trip of mine. All the other parents were moms, but I remember being so proud to have my dad along. I can't remember where we went, but I do remember sitting on the bus with him.

ALEX, 23, GREEN BAY, WISCONSIN

I will never forget the day my father taught me how to drive a car. I had heard friends' stories of their disastrous driving lessons, but my father was full of confidence, saying I would do just fine.

We started on empty back roads, practicing starting, stopping, turning. Dad kept me heading toward busier and busier streets, saying I was doing great and presenting more driving challenges as soon as he thought I could handle them.

After my first ninety minutes behind the wheel, Dad innocently said to take a left. Next thing I knew, he had me merging onto the Long Island Expressway into a sea of cars that was zooming along a parkway renowned for its traffic! Dad calmly said I would do fine, and I did.

When we returned home to my curious and concerned mother, Dad said simply, "She knows how to drive!" My Dad thinks I can do anything, and with him I can.

SHERI, 49, LAKE BUENA VISTA, FLORIDA

Dad collects things. Even the word *things* is magic to him. He's never owned a store called "Bob's Things-n-Stuff," but he could.

Dad's got thirty years' worth of record albums, plus cassette tapes and CDs—he loves music in all forms. Ditto for books. And, yes, videos—both bought and taped from TV, a collection that rivals that of any independent video store.

Dad loves Americana, be it a six-foot plastic lawn snowman or a crocheted pumpkin or a velour rug of Elvis Presley. Then there are random items that we don't need now—but might need someday. Or maybe a friend will need someday. Like an art easel, golf clubs, a bread maker, a dollhouse . . .

On the wall in our garage are framed black-and-white photographs of relatives from long ago—that is, relatives of the people who sold them at a yard sale.

Life's big mystery for Dad is "What's inside that second-hand store that I don't yet have?"

HAYES, 17, SPRINGFIELD, OREGON

Years ago, my sister planned her wedding for December 30. This was her second marriage, his first. She was living in Florida, near Mom and Dad. I was in New York.

I was involved in an off-Broadway play that was scheduled to open right after the New Year, and I did not know how I could break away so close to an opening. Dad, however, would not take no for an answer.

Over the course of several weeks prior to the wedding, Dad would call me up to try to convince me to go. Each time, I explained the situation to him. When he called on Christmas, Dad asked one more time, adding, "You have to be there."

"Why?"

"Because you have to give her away."

"Why do I have to give her away? I'm her brother. You're her father. It's your responsibility to give her away."

"Hell, son, I done gave her away once. . . . They gave her back."

SHAWN, 58, WEST PALM BEACH, FLORIDA

'Ve learned a lot from my father, both from his actions and from his advice. Such as:

If you didn't make the meal, then do the dishes.

Ask for directions. It saves time.

Don't put off 'til tomorrow what you can put off to the next day.

When in doubt, relax!

Even if you're just above average intelligence, that still makes you smarter than over 2.5 billion people on the planet.

KOLYA, 16, DES MOINES, IOWA

I telephone to my father, now in the early stages of Alzheimer's. My daughter has a question about her chemistry homework, and I am wondering if he will be able to help. I phrase it simply, but still he is silent, unable to access the most basic of information that made up most of his career.

It brings me back to my own high school chemistry days, when covalent bonds and ionic charges threatened to overwhelm me. One Sunday, my father spent the entire afternoon unraveling my questions.

"What does that mean?" I remember asking. "Why does that happen?" and "How does it work?" I batted one question after another at my father, who sat beside me at our kitchen table, munching an apple. It took hours before I was comfortable with his answers and confident that I understood. But after that, I really did understand, and for the rest of the year, I got A's on all my tests.

SUSAN, 49, MOUNT KISCO, NEW YORK

My father worked hard all his life, getting up at three A.M. and working until dusk at the service station he owned with his brother. One day, he announced he'd "had it" with work and asked his brother to buy him out. Though my brothers and I were grown, married with new babies, it still seemed premature.

But Dad wanted to relax, to travel all around the United States and see famous sights. The pile of baby-sized state T-shirts our new son and niece received spelled out Mom and Dad's route cross-country. They were in Arizona when they found out Dad's mother, in Florida, was quite ill. They drove straight to her side, rented an apartment, and stayed with her for two months, until she died. One month after returning home, Mom and Dad took off again—this time for Alaska.

I'm glad Dad followed his instincts to fulfill some dreams while he was still energetic and healthy, because he died of cancer at age sixty-five.

STEVEN, 43, LAS VEGAS, NEVADA

Dad was a big ice-hockey player when he was young, and he passed the love of the sport on to me when I was barely old enough to hold a stick. We have hours' and years' worth of videos of the two of us playing on our driveway and the ice pond. By age seven, I was on a team; Dad would practice with me and cheer at the games.

I started getting sick of hockey at around age ten, but I was not mature enough to tell Dad, who was my team's coach. I played that season and the next three. All those freezing, dark, early mornings going to practice or away games. Hockey camp. The sweaty smell of the car from all my equipment. Dad supporting me all the way. My guilt.

Just before high school, I told Dad I wanted to try out for basketball. He was shocked and disappointed. Trouble was, I was too inexperienced at basketball to make the team.

CHRIS, 29, MILWAUKEE, WISCONSIN

Every year for our birthdays, Dad would give us a handmade card with money in it, but he made it a game to guess how much. When we opened the card up, there was a tiny diamond cut in the center fold. In the diamond, you could see one eye, and it was either George Washington's eye on the one-dollar bill, Abraham Lincoln's eye on the five-dollar bill, or Alexander Hamilton's eye on the ten-dollar bill. We had to guess whose eye, and then open the card a certain way to see if we were right.

AARON, 49, KNOXVILLE, TENNESSEE

Dad grew up on a farm. One time, he was playing baseball out in a big field with some friends. He rounded third base and started heading home to score the first run. Someone threw the ball to the pitcher. Dad slid into home plate—and into an enormous pile of cow dung.

JACK, 16, PORTSMOUTH, NEW HAMPSHIRE

My dad's a doctor and when he comes home every night, I ask him, "Did you do any surgery today?" and usually he says, "No, I just took care of people's colds." When he says, "Yes," my brother really, really likes it, but I have to put my hands over my ears, because he tells the parts of the body he took out.

I like to visit his office near the hospital. It's small, with pictures of me and the rest of the family. Underneath his desk are brown paper bags filled with cookies. I don't know how he gets all these bags, but he always has good stuff.

EMMA, 6, LANSING, MICHIGAN

Humor was prized in my family, and we had stacks of it—in the form of sixteen-inch, heavy black records of Bob Hope's USO shows performed during World War II. Dad had brought these records back from the war—all the way from the tiny Japanese island of Kwajalein, where he worked at a radio control tower, signaling planes.

Perhaps they played these records during lulls in the action. But as his troop was leaving the island, Dad realized these records would just be left behind, so he took them. They were big and heavy, and the only way to board their aircraft carrier at sea was to climb up netting strung over the side. How he got up the side of that ship with those records under one arm is a mystery.

Dad must have known the records were worth the trouble, especially years later, hearing his children laugh over and over as we played those war relics down in our basement.

ALLEN, 50, LUBBOCK, TEXAS

I was the oldest of six children and often broke ground with my parents. Once, after a less-than-stellar decision on my part, my dad admonished me: "I don't have many material things to give you or your sisters or brother," he said. "The one thing I have worked hard for and can give any of you is your last name. If you bring shame on our family name, you lose that reputation not only for yourself but take it from everyone else in the family."

This talk was a defining moment in my life. I grew up that day and began looking at all my choices with a new seriousness and moral clarity that went beyond just me and what I wanted. I have let those words be a guiding principle of my life and actions ever since.

Michael, 43, Washington, D.C.

I had lunch with my dad at a restaurant one afternoon, and I have never appreciated that simple activity more. We were in my hometown, where I now work at my first postcollege job.

Dad normally works in New York City, but he did not go in that day: It was September 12, 2001, the day after the World Trade Center attacks, and Mayor Giuliani had asked people not to go into the city if they didn't have to. That morning, in our town, there were men everywhere, walking with their wives, dropping off kids at school, clusters of them having coffee outside at Starbucks. It felt strange, but reassuring, to see all those dads. Normally, the town is mostly women and children between nine and five on weekdays.

Sitting at the restaurant table across from Dad, I savored his presence, thinking of the many families where a dad would no longer be coming home. I was so lucky to have mine.

MAYA, 23, FORT LEE, NEW JERSEY

❖ ❖ ❖ ❖ ❖ ❖ 94 ❖ ❖ ❖ ❖ ❖ ❖

Dad was an elementary school teacher for twenty-four years. During that time, he taught second, fourth, and fifth grades, and then, when I hit sixth grade, he moved there, too (but not at my school). We laughed about being in sixth grade together. Dad loved sixth grade and was the "cool" teacher to get.

I figured Dad would just teach sixth grade until retirement. But two years ago, Dad's school ended the sixth grade and moved it to the middle school, which offered Dad eighth-grade social studies. I wondered how he would deal with this change, if he would take early retirement.

Instead, Dad took the job. It was hard at first. He was no longer "king." He didn't know the school or other teachers and had to learn a new curriculum.

And the amazing thing was, he said it was the best thing that could ever have happened to him. Though Dad was never my teacher, he taught me a lot about life.

ERIK, 36, NASHVILLE, TENNESSEE

My dad has many endearing qualities, but humility is not one of them. Fortunately, Mom can usually see through all that.

So, Mom and Dad are on an elevator heading to the lobby of the building where they had just had dinner with friends. The elevator stops, my mother gets out, but seeing that it's not the lobby, comes back into the elevator. My father teases her mercilessly—citing age, bad eyes, and general cluelessness for having made such a stupid mistake.

Meanwhile, the elevator stops again and Dad steps out— then, *argh!* he realizes that it's not the lobby! My mother says nothing, just smiles. Dad is tormented: He can't admit he's made the same mistake, and far be it from him to apologize. But Dad *can* rationalize: "Well, mine didn't count, you know. I only took two steps out," he says, "while you took several more!"

SOUSKI, 39, ROCHESTER, MINNESOTA

My dad was always so different from other dads. He was about twenty years older and, being from Italy, had a thick accent. Surprisingly, I wasn't embarrassed about these things—rather, I felt all the more proud of him. I loved to hear him tell his "immigrant story," about coming to New York in 1921 and not knowing what he was going to do with his life.

Before coming here, Dad was trained professionally in opera. Over here, Dad took on some students and in time became a well-known coach, with some of his students becoming famous in the industry. Later, Dad took another of his passions—food—and created a restaurant where the waiters and waitresses would sing opera during dinner. This restaurant became our family's livelihood—and life—for decades and was a real tribute to my dad's talents, passions, and love of people.

TILDE, 44, SAN TERENZO, ITALY

My father played the piano. His music was that of the Frank Sinatra fifties and sixties; Broadway show tunes; and the orchestra leader Lester Lanin. But he was able to lend his own style and interpretation to anything. Dad played often—before dinner, on weekends, while waiting for Mom to finish dressing before they went out in the evening.

Dad learned the piano from his mother, herself an accomplished pianist. He earned his first pair of skis playing in some low-rent bar in Idaho; after the war, he played in cafés along the Riviera—the only war story he liked to tell.

Dad played because he loved to, and his friends and family loved to hear him. Dad died fifteen years ago, but when I close my eyes and listen, I can still hear him playing. His music is the sound track to my childhood and memories of home.

JOANNA, 47, CHARLOTTE, NORTH CAROLINA

May 1st is May Day, which not many people either know about or celebrate, but Dad was one who knew and did. As a child and young girl, I received a May basket filled with sweets and flowers from Dad every year.

Dad continued this tradition with my three children. He lived nearby and every May 1st he'd come over with three beautiful baskets and put them on our doorstep. The kids would find the baskets waiting for them before they left for school.

When it was time for my eldest child to go away to college, Dad wondered if the three were getting too old for the May baskets. He decided they weren't and sent my daughter's to her by mail.

ANN, 70, NEWPORT NEWS, VIRGINIA

Back in elementary school, getting lice was one of the things I dreaded most. Kids cried, even my kindergarten teacher cried, when she herself had to be sent home. Having those horrible bugs in your hair meant scrubbing it with a smelly rinse that stung, having someone pick through your hair for hours, and having your favorite stuffed animals sealed up for weeks in a plastic bag. With my long hair that I loved to wear down, I was a perfect target. And when I got lice, Mom freaked out and Dad took charge.

As Dad rinsed my hair, he spoke gently to calm me down. But then he took me, and even my lice-free sister, straight to the hair parlor—and ordered our hair cut short, up to our ears! We screamed and sobbed. Dad just told us how beautiful we looked . . . and strangely, after my anger wore off, I saw what he meant. Everyone complimented me and I saw myself in a new light.

KAITLYN, 18, WASHINGTON, D.C.

My father was always something of an eccentric, though I didn't see him that way when I was young. So I didn't think anything of the day my dad bought an old school bus. Dad had a plan for this bus: He took out most of the seats and built bunk beds. The seats he kept attached were in the center of the bus, where he added a table. Then he painted the whole thing a brilliant lime green. This was our family camper.

This lime-green behemoth—which could carry fifty schoolchildren but which Dad fitted to carry just us five—was also our only means of transportation on those trips. This meant that just going out to a Wendy's or McDonald's or the beach meant getting on the bus, bouncing along the street and in traffic, and then parking it in the lot (Mom always got out to direct).

At the time, I thought this was normal. Only now do I think . . . how bizarre!

JUDY, 37, LARCHMONT, NEW YORK

My parents divorced when I was thirteen years old, and I lived with my mother. Within a year, Dad had remarried and—*boom!*—suddenly they had a new baby boy named Justin.

The weird thing was, the same thing had happened with my best friend, Mike, a few years before. That's why my new baby brother terrified me—because I saw that after Mike's half-brother was born, Mike's dad and his new family moved away and Mike barely ever saw his dad.

But I've been lucky. Dad stayed nearby and, even though it was sometimes hard for Mom, he and my stepmother, Sasha, have included me in almost every phase of their and Justin's life. The weekends, vacations, birthdays, and holidays over the years have kept us a solid family. Justin even came to visit me at college (he was in sixth grade at the time), and I couldn't have been prouder.

MATTHEW, 25, HAZELWOOD, MISSOURI

D ad was luckier than his older sisters, who, as young children in Austria-Hungary, had to flee their native village to escape anti-Jewish violence. Sometimes, the family separated as they fled, though they eventually found each other and later settled in the tiny village of Buczacz (since wiped out). Dad was born there, in 1918, the second youngest of five.

Grandpa came to New York in 1925 and worked whatever jobs he could get until he could pay for the rest of the family to come over. Dad was ten years old when he passed through Ellis Island and on to the Bronx. His father eventually owned five area grocery stores; even though the depression nearly wiped Grandpa out, Dad was still able to go on to college and law school.

Dad's favorite story was how he met my mother: In the early 1940s, Dad attended a dance for the Sons of Buczacz, where he fell in love with a local young woman whose mother was from Buczacz. They married and produced a son, me.

MITCH, 50, FLAGSTAFF, ARIZONA

My mother was from a working-class neighborhood in The Bronx and my dad was from a more well-to-do section of Manhattan. When they were first dating, my dad would dress up in his finest suit to go visit my mom. At that time, white linen suits were all the rage on the Upper East Side, and Dad sported his with pride. However, upon arrival in The Bronx, Dad would be perceived differently, with the neighborhood kids announcing his arrival with: "Hey, the Good Humor man's here!"

LINDA, 62, NEW YORK, NEW YORK

My dad loved trains. Loved the look of them, loved riding in them. Loved making model trains. For most of Dad's life, trains were the only way to travel far distances, still part of the golden age of trains. By the time that age ended, I was a young man and already caught up in my father's passion for tracks, engines, passenger cars, and rail cars—both real and model. In fact, my wife and I chose the location for our house by the distance it was from the train tracks, separated by woods.

My son and I built model train cars and tracks together, and I suppose I have handed down the train passion to him. He, in turn, has passed this on to his wife and their children.

I still have a railroad room up in my attic. Some of the models are ones Dad made—handcrafted boxcars whose numbers are actually birth dates and anniversaries of family members. I can't think of a finer legacy.

DAVE, 73, SHELBURNE FALLS, MASSACHUSETTS

Dad has many outstanding qualities. But one quality that stands out big is a certain four-letter word: *L-A-Z-Y.* The dominant force of his life is figuring out how to do something using the least possible amount of energy.

Dad hates to bend over. This I learned as a toddler, watching Dad pick up my toys with a cherry picker. Shovel snow? Not Dad and his super-duper snowblower. Rake leaves? Not with his tornado-force leaf blower.

Every year, Dad goes to yard sales to find power tools, and he is little-boyishly thrilled every time he finds an upgrade to some tool he has. Last time I went with him, he bought a child's wagon. "Dad, I'm in college!" I laughed. He said, "It's not for you—it's to put the paper recycling bin on, so I don't have to lift it."

With our remotes, timers, cell phones, etc., our house is a Gadget-o-rama. The one thing Dad doesn't have, but still wants, is a robot to bring him a beer from the fridge.

BRIGITTE, 21, WILMINGTON, DELAWARE

My father has the gift of gab, has a great sense of humor, and is full of funny one-liners and jokes. But when I was a little boy and asked him to make up a bedtime story, he drew a blank. For him, making up stories was excruciatingly hard. The one and only story he ever thought of was called "Frank, the Hot Dog Boy," about a boy who looked like a hot dog and played baseball and quite *frankly* had some pretty lame adventures.

NICK, 18, SIOUX FALLS, SOUTH DAKOTA

Dad expected dinner to be served to him every night, though this wasn't always possible. When I was in middle school, Mom started a small business of her own and was sometimes out when Dad got home. She would leave him a plate with everything ready to be warmed up in the microwave, but Dad's response was, "I guess I have to get my own dinner tonight."

My sister and I would have to convince him that all he had to do was warm up the plate. That Mom had actually made a very nice dinner but she just wasn't there to serve it. "This isn't the fifties," we'd remind him. "Or the Stone Age." He'd try to get one of us to wash his dish afterward. Sometimes we'd give in; sometimes the plate just lay in the sink.

On my last visit home, I saw a frozen dinner in the freezer —wow! Dad could now make himself an emergency supper, Mom said proudly. For Dad, that's progress.

LIA, 19, CHESTERFIELD, MISSOURI

I was an only child, growing up not far from New York City. On the weekends, Dad, a great art lover, would take me to visit museums—either the Metropolitan Museum of Art or the Museum of Modern Art or the contemporary, circular Guggenheim. "Oh, *ugh!*" was my response. I was his captive and desperately wished that I had a sibling or two with whom to share the misery.

Unconsciously, however, these museum visits had a strong impact on my life, by my own choosing. I majored in art history in college and landed my first job out of college at the prestigious Fogg Art Museum in Cambridge. Needless to say, Dad was thrilled.

Though I have since left the art field professionally, art is still a love of mine, linked indelibly to Dad.

LISA, 45, EAST GREENWICH, RHODE ISLAND

When my sister and I were young, we went to Sweden (from our home in Norway) for a week every winter to learn how to ski. Mama and Papa already knew how, so they put us in ski school, starting at the bunny hill.

One afternoon, as Papa was heading down to the bottom, he spotted us on the beginner slope and skied on over. The ski lift for us beginners was a long pole with a hook, called a J-bar. To get up the hill, you pull the bar down, lean forward, and let it pull you up the hill on your skis.

Papa saw that and felt he had to tell us young ones how it should be used. He got in line and when it was his turn, he *sat* on it! He immediately fell down in a cloud of snow, with the lift operators and a crowd of kids staring at him. My sister and I lowered our heads, pretending not to know him, and zoomed up the J-bar past him.

MARIAN, 23, TRONDHEIM, NORWAY

When I was thirteen years old, my dad took my brother, mother, and me on a long weekend excursion from our home in Massachusetts to south-central Canada, to see the famous Dionne quintuplets. This was 1938. There were no highways then, only roads; few cars; and no speed limits. Afterward, because we were "in the neighborhood," according to Dad, we all drove hours and hours farther to Yellowstone National Park.

Inspired by that trip, the next summer Dad took us cross-country again: In the black Packard, we drove 12,000 miles through thirty states in five weeks. We saw everything—petrified forests, the Grand Canyon, Hollywood, and much more. I still have the map of our route, my travel journal, postcards, and brochures.

What Dad's trips did was plant a lifelong love of going to different places, be they near or far, to learn and see new things. I just get in the car and off I go!

DOROTHY, 76, PUNTA GORDA, FLORIDA

When I was home on college break last year, my dad told me I was washing the dishes wrong. First of all, he pointed out, I didn't need to use a steel wool pad on china plates—it scratched the heck out of them. He handed me a proper dish-washing sponge. Second, he said, I was wasting water as I washed, that I didn't need to keep the water running the whole time, and he showed me a better way to wash. I took his suggestions in stride, figuring Dad's approaching retirement was making him cranky.

A year later now, I find myself living in a group house with people whose ways of doing things never seem as good as my way. And with our area in a severe drought, I'm very water conscious as I wash the dishes, and even more so as I watch my housemates waste water. Dad, now I feel your pain.

MIKE, 22, GREAT FALLS, MONTANA

My father's prized possessions were two objects that his dad had given him. My grandfather fought in the Civil War and was shot at the Battle of Vicksburg. As family legend has it, he dug the musket ball out of his stomach with an ivory-handled knife and lived to tell the tale.

The musket ball was dust colored and about as big as a medium-sized marble. That musket ball and the bloodstained knife that saved Grandpa were always on Papa's large office bureau. As little children, we admired these objects greatly because Papa did. But the romance of war disappeared when, as a child, I saw soldiers—including Papa—returning from the Great War. However, Papa had taken the musket ball off to war with him for good luck, and since he was lucky enough to come back in one piece, maybe there was something to it.

MYRTLE, 92, FAIRFAX, VIRGINIA

My father liked animals, but he didn't have very much respect for their intelligence. On a trip to Benson's Wild Animal Farm, we went into the elephant house to see the baby elephants.

Each small elephant had his or her own stall, outside of which stood a bucket of fresh sawdust. Dad had a bag of unshelled peanuts. He started to offer some to a baby elephant, when the rest of us asked, "Do they eat the shells, too?"

"They'll never know the difference," Dad replied, and he offered up a handful of unshelled peanuts.

The baby elephant picked the peanuts up with his trunk and put them in his mouth. After a few seconds, the elephant reached into the bucket of sawdust with his trunk, then showered my father—and only my father—with sawdust. My father sputtered and we roared. And the sawdust did not come out of my dad's sweater until after the next wash day.

CAROL, 70, POINT PLEASANT, NEW JERSEY

My dad's one indulgence was a red sports car, a convertible, and when my three sisters and I were young, we would pile into the back, top down, and Dad would take us to get ice cream. But rather than waiting for us to decide on a flavor, Dad invented a game: We four girls would wait outside the ice-cream shop and Dad would emerge a few minutes later with a surprise for each of us. He made it seem like getting a surprise flavor (even one we might not like) was a real treat.

As we clambered back into the car, Dad would make sure no ice cream would drip onto his four-wheeled treasure by checking each of our cones. If one of ours was too messy, he'd say, "Let me clean that off for you," and then would lick into shape what seemed like half the cone. No matter what, it was always a delicious, lighthearted trip with Dad.

Lucy, 51, North Scituate, Rhode Island

Dad always made time for my sister, brother, me, and a lot of other kids growing up in my hometown. He was a basketball and football coach, baseball umpire, football equipment manager, and Cub Scout leader—along with a few other titles that he volunteered for, to help out the community.

One of my best memories is when he used to help me with my newspaper route. He would wake me at five-thirty every morning, bring the newspapers in off the sidewalk, and make me breakfast. Then off I would go on my bike, unless it was raining or snowing: Then Dad would drive me.

On Sunday mornings, Dad and I would load up the station wagon with over a hundred extra-big papers to be delivered. The radio station was always WNEW from New York City, and the program was always Jonathan Schwartz playing Frank Sinatra. I still have a fondness for Sinatra because of the memory of having Dad all to myself on those Sunday mornings.

RICHARD, 43, COMPTON, MARYLAND

It was New Year's Eve, 1966, when my very sick mother was taken away in the ambulance. My father wasn't one for putting up with other people's health problems, so if my mother had not been feeling well, no one would have mentioned it.

I can see my twelve-year-old self and my ten-year-old brother, Patrick, watching as she was taken away. My father had never spent any time alone with us, much less given us something to eat. We ended up going to the Old Westbury Inn, a rather fancy establishment, which helped take my mind off my mother.

New Year's Eve was in full swing. My father made a valiant attempt at diverting us, and he succeeded with me. He ordered a martini and I was allowed a Shirley Temple—my first cocktail. I cannot remember what my brother ordered, but it all became irrelevant, because shortly afterward, Patrick threw up on the table and that put an end to the evening. My mother recovered.

MARIANNE, 48, LONDON, ENGLAND

My father had a round face, sparkly eyes, and a scar that started at one ear, ran across his neck, and almost reached the other ear. He looked like he had nearly been beheaded in a sword fight.

Dad never liked to talk about his childhood, growing up in a war-torn border town between Poland and Russia in the years before the revolution. But he did tell one story, the story of his scar, which never seemed to embarrass him. Instead, he wore it proudly and had for nearly his whole life.

When Dad was three, he got tuberculosis of the neck from drinking bad milk. After he was operated on, my grandmother strapped him to her back and walked for three days to reach Odessa, where she packed him in the city's special black mud so he would heal.

JACKIE, 50, HATTIESBURG, MISSISSIPPI

Dad was once in an elevator at the Plaza Hotel in New York City when Shaquille O'Neal got on. As Dad describes it, he was suddenly flattened against the elevator wall by the extra crush of people, not just Shaq. Still, to this day, I cannot get over that Dad was so close to one of the greatest basketball players of all time and did not get his autograph!

OLIVER, 10, FULTON, GEORGIA

Of the many things I've learned from my dad, one is that part of being a parent is the unbearable pain he feels when his child says, "Dad, I'm so sad." He feels a powerlessness so acute that he is left dumbstruck. Another thing I've learned is that Dad loves life with every fiber of his being.

LESLIE, 39, NEW YORK, NEW YORK

My dad is a landscaper, and growing up, one thing I liked about his line of work was that he was always buying used trucks, all the same type, so he could borrow parts from one to fix another. It was cool having all those trucks in our yard.

As my sixteenth birthday approached, Dad offered me one of the cars we had. I turned him down; I was really hoping for a sports car. Dad shook his head (spoiled son, he probably thought), but I hoped he'd change his mind.

On my birthday—wow! There it was, the car of my dreams—except it had no engine! That I had to supply. Little by little, I learned what parts I needed and how to put them together. It took years to finish; by then, I wasn't even living at home, and Dad ended up using the car.

Still, I learned how to put together a car engine. And I also learned to be careful what you wish for.

ELISEO, 28, SAN CLEMENTE, CALIFORNIA

My father, a Frenchman, was an actor, both in theater and film, though he preferred the stage. The time I spent with him was usually backstage, among the costumes, scenery, and fellow actors.

One time, one of the children in a play he was in called in sick at the last minute, and I got to substitute. I had seen the rehearsals enough to know the part, yet the thing that made it most thrilling was to be in the same play as my father.

ANTONIA, 41, PARIS, FRANCE

My dad was a strong role model for leadership. He encouraged us all to believe in what we wanted and to aim high to achieve it. In high school, I wanted to be a class officer. When I rehearsed my self-written speech, he said to change the line "If I am elected . . ." to "When I am your secretary . . ." As I gave my speech, I shut my eyes, terrified at the look on my classmates' faces as I spoke. But I won. I hope I can teach my own children the same thing: that if they want something, they must aim high, assert themselves, and go for it.

GAIL, 52, NAPERVILLE, ILLINOIS

There is a certain doorway in Glen Cove, New York, that takes me back to my childhood. The door leads to an office vestibule, and when I go back and visit, the smell of that vestibule is unchanged since the days my dad had a doctor's office on the second floor. I close my eyes and can hear my shoes clattering up the staircase. . . .

Once inside Dad's office, I sit quietly in the waiting area with the other patients. When Dad comes out from being with a patient, he's so happy and proud to see me, he introduces me to all his patients: "This is my lovely daughter, Debbie." He makes it easy to greet everyone and I can tell they think the world of my father.

Before I go, especially if I'm with friends, Dad tucks some dollar bills in my pocket so we can go buy ourselves a treat.

DEBBIE, 45, LARCHMONT, NEW YORK

I'm twenty-six years old, the same age Dad was when I was born. I never realized, until recently, how young Dad was when he became a father. Just before I was born, Dad dropped out of graduate school. He was studying to be an actor and always just muttered something about not having what it took to be one. He often said, and I figured he was just being corny, that the best role in life was to be a dad and husband—a role that also required a steady income. I don't know if I could be as positive and selfless about giving up some dream like that at my age. It would be tough—but Dad never let on if it was.

GAETANO, 26, EVERETT, WASHINGTON

I 'd always wanted a dog, but my parents said the landlord didn't allow pets. I was never sure if they'd really asked or if they just didn't want the responsibility.

When we moved to our own house on Long Island in 1971, there was no commercial garbage pickup and we had to go to the dump. There was a dog pound on the same road.

Soon after we moved, we were on our way back from the dump, when Dad pulled the car into the dog pound. "Let's just have a look," he said. Right.

Amid the yelping dogs in their too-small cages, we noticed a small gray dog, huddled in the back of the cage, too scared to bark, yelp, or even whimper. The attendant opened the cage for us and put the shaking puppy in my arms.

We named her Buffy.

Mom wasn't thrilled, but when Dad and I went out to get dog food, Buffy curled herself under Mom's ironing board. She was a good dog.

Carol, 50, Grahamsville, New York

The happiest day of my life was when you were born." Dad tells me that, no joke, several times a month.

ELLEN, 26, WASHINGTON, D.C.

We lived on the West Side of Manhattan, where my parents had a men's store called "Gentlemen's Hats." My dad created and cleaned hats as well as sold clothing and accessories.

Dad was an artist in vision and talented in his creation. His craftsmanship was well known and he developed a clientele outside of New York. The one customer that sticks in my mind was a cowboy in Texas. Every six months, this cowboy had my dad make and send him a silver-and-white cowboy hat. Into this hat, Dad poured all his creativity, never charging him the cost of his labor—or it would have been unaffordable. From my dad (and the cowboy), I learned the meaning of "labor of love."

EVA, 58, TEANECK, NEW JERSEY

My father has spent his entire life giving to the needy, while unapologetically not giving to his family. As a parent, I've found it difficult to go through so many birthdays and Christmases with never a gift from him. However, I know Dad has given in meaningful ways to others—but it was a true watershed when I recently found myself on his receiving end.

I was witness to the September 11th attacks on the World Trade Center, and a few weeks later, I lost my position with a company I'd been with for fourteen years. Several months later, I went to my mailbox and found a parcel addressed to me from my father. I could not have been more stunned.

In it was a handwritten note and two books—a Bible and a book about finding peace, based on Psalm 23. This gift, with its perfect messages for right now, is more appreciated than any gift I have ever received.

LAURA, 45, LARCHMONT, NEW YORK

When I was a baby, my mom decided to go shopping with her mother. I was left at home for the first time with my grandfather and dad. Sometime during the day, they had to change my diaper, which was new for Dad. He was so proud of that accomplishment, he kept going and got me dressed.

When my mom and grandmother got home, they took one look at me and burst out laughing, but Dad and Grandpa could not see what was so funny.

It turned out that when Dad put on my clothes, he put both of my legs into one pant leg. And for the hours until my mom and grandma got home, neither one ever even noticed.

ISABELLE, 12, SAN DIEGO, CALIFORNIA

One Christmas vacation when I was still in high school, my sister, Lynn, came home from college for the holidays. Lynn, my Mom, and I were all in the kitchen, busily yakking away, when our father, a quiet man, entered and calmly said, "There appears to be a conflagration in the living room," then left the kitchen.

Engrossed in our own conversation, we paid little attention, until there was a pause, during which I turned to my mother and asked, "What is a conflagration?" She looked at me and answered, "A fire."

Finally realizing what Pop had said, we all rushed into the living room to find him cleaning up what remained of a Christmas decoration that Mom had placed around a candle. He laughed and told us he had been wondering how long it was going to take us to hear what he had said.

I guess what I'm still learning about Pop is: When he speaks—even in his calm, gentle voice—*listen!*

SUSAN, 50, WOODLAND PARK, COLORADO

When I was ten, my father took my sister and me to a drive-in near our home in Santa Monica to see the remake of *King Kong*. The sight of that huge mechanical ape hand wrapping around a screaming Jessica Lange enthralled me.

Dad wasn't supposed to take us to "those" movies (as my mother called them). She preferred lighter, age-appropriate fare, like *Bedknobs and Broomsticks*. But my parents had separated when I was five, and this was just one of my father's ploys to win us over. Weekend visits often consisted of pizzas, toy stores, and forbidden movies: *The Spy Who Loved Me*, *Jaws*, *Saturday Night Fever*.

"Remember, don't tell your mother about seeing this movie," my dad would call to us as we headed toward the drive-in's dirty, rusty playground in our Dr. Denton feety pajamas.

Keeping their secrets allowed us to believe that a bond still existed between the two of them, and that our loyalty was what held us all together.

ROB, 33, NEW YORK, NEW YORK

I couldn't sleep because the cannibals were coming for me. From my bedroom, I snaked my way through our dark house to the safety of the family room. The room was filled with light, the sounds of John Wayne saving someone—and my father, a couch of a man. He sat me on his lap and opened an atlas.

"Here is South America, here is Arizona," he said, drawing a line with his finger. Cannibals, he explained, didn't have jobs, so they had no money to pay for plane tickets or taxi rides. "If they had money," he continued, "they would have to get from the jungle to a major airport and fly from there to Phoenix," where we lived. "They won't have driver's licenses, so they would need to hire a taxi. It's four hours round-trip. Most drivers won't do that."

By the time he explained passports, I knew that the cannibals wouldn't come for me. I began to sleep soundly again. Until I learned about quicksand.

MARLEY, 30, TUCSON, ARIZONA

My dad showed me the world. First, through the light-up globe on a stand that he placed in our family room. Later, through exotic travels over several summers with him, my mom, and my four siblings—to the South Pacific, the Seychelles, Micronesia, Indonesia—and more.

He was simply a man from northern Illinois who enjoyed exploring the world with his family. And my dad prized these trips, not for the souvenirs we brought back, but for the happy times we experienced far from home, together.

BETH, 42, EVANSTON, ILLINOIS

In his day, my dad was known unofficially as the mayor of Greenwich Village, because he knew everyone and everyone knew him. He was a dapper man, an Italian, and a master tailor by profession.

In his eighties and quite ill, Dad was at the hospital, awaiting surgery. I went into intensive care to see him, and he asked if I could find a mirror.

"What for?" I asked.

"Well, by the time I recover from the operation, a few days will have passed," he explained. "I'll be a little less scruffy if I shave now."

The nurses did not have a mirror, so Dad ended up using the mirror on my lipstick holder, which made us all laugh. Still, he pulled through the surgery just as planned, and I don't remember a five o'clock shadow I was ever happier to see.

Antoinette, 78, Larchmont, New York

I had my first dance with my father when I was three years old. My two older sisters (they were five and seven) and I were on vacation with my parents, and one night we ate at a place with a band and a dance floor. After first dancing with my mom, Dad then asked one sister, who said, "Oh, no, Daddy, I'd be too embarrassed." My other sister said the same thing. But I said, "I'll dance with you, Daddy!"

Dad was surprised and for a moment not sure how to dance with a three-year-old. Then he scooped me up in his arms and waltzed me around the floor. What a lovely beginning to dancing with Dad.

MARIA, 37, DAYTON, OHIO

Dad would take my two older brothers and me out to the sand dunes near our house. We had a dune buggy that he'd bought us and we would all take turns. My brothers would fight over who went longer and who got to ride more. I used to give up my turn so I could sit with my dad.

One evening, there was a brilliant red sunset over the dunes, and the song "Dust in the Wind" came on the radio. Whenever I hear that song now, it brings me right back to the dunes with my dad.

JARED, 30, BOSTON, MASSACHUSETTS

True love is often expressed through unexpected gestures. On a family vacation years ago, Dad proved his devotion to mom with a can of soup. After a long day of traveling, we were exhausted. And Mom was ill. What we thought had been motion sickness turned out to be a terrible stomach virus. Dad put her to bed and scoured the area for a twenty-four-hour convenience store to buy some chicken broth to help settle her stomach. He came back with a dented can (the last in the store), which he managed to open with several different tools on his multipurpose pocketknife. There was no hot plate in our room, and the hotel's restaurant had closed.

In his determination to help nurse Mom back to health, he returned to our rental car, popped the hood, and placed the can on the engine. He soon returned with a steaming can of broth, which mom sipped from the empty ice bucket in our room. Mom recovered quickly, thanks to Dad's "souper" idea.

LAURA, 30, BROOKLYN, NEW YORK

My father brought into my life the love for what is different, the love of adventure, and a desire to learn from other cultures. I am forever grateful for it.

It all started when I was eight years old and my father began traveling to Somalia from Italy every winter. He went for vacation, also visiting cousins who had banana plantations there, and brought home stories and pictures. The women were stunning and wore beautiful *futas*.

Then there were the pictures of my father holding a monkey or showing off his latest kill. My father loved nature and the wild as well as fishing and hunting—a product of his time, I believe.

What I missed most with my dad was quality time. But that was forgotten when I saw the expression in his eyes the day I came home from New York with my college degree from Fordham University. I was forty and he was eighty and we were father and daughter.

MARIUCCIA, 56, BELIZE CITY, BELIZE

My husband and I were living in Chicago, when my brother, then a struggling intern, came to a medical conference in town. Though he could have stayed at the luxurious Drake Hotel, he chose to stay with us. I assumed "pocketing" the money for the hotel was behind his decision, and when I asked him how much he'd make that way, he seemed surprised. He said he was staying with us so we could spend more time together, and he'd save the hospital money. I was impressed and proud of my brother. I wondered where, in a world that regularly "works the system," he had learned such integrity.

Months later, I went out to dinner with my dad. My meal included the "make-your-own sundae," and knowing how much Dad loves ice cream, I asked him if he'd like me to sneak him some. He gave me a strange look and said "No, it doesn't come with my meal." I knew right then where my brother had gotten his integrity!

AMY, 45, ALLEN, TEXAS

Whenever I go to the beach, which is something I love to do, I think of my dad. One of my earliest memories is of going into the waves with him—and I don't think I've ever felt as safe or serene since. There was the water, all cold, with the white foam, and the waves crashing, and it was so exhilarating. And there was Dad right near me, ready to catch me if I fell and who would never let me drown.

BOBBIE, 50, MOUNT PLEASANT, SOUTH CAROLINA

One year, Dad was seized with the idea of showing my sisters and me the West. Mom went along with it, but it was Dad's trip. In Denver, we rented an RV and for a few hours, maybe almost a day, everything was great. The mountains were spectacular, the weather nice, etc. Then we started using the RV's shower and turning on the air-conditioning. That's when the flooding started.

Water from the cooling pipes and the shower started leaking inside the RV—and not just in little trickles, but enough to slosh from side to side whenever we turned a corner. Dad started singing camp songs, even sailing songs (including one about the *Titanic*), from the wheel, trying to keep our spirits up until we got to our next stop.

That first leaky night, Dad took a pan and started scooping up some of the water. Then he opened the door and threw it out—right onto me. This was the kind of trip that only gets funny in hindsight.

ELANA, 24, PORTSMOUTH, NEW HAMPSHIRE

My dad went to college in upstate New York in the early sixties. Back then, there wasn't much to do outside of class, but Dad came up with some interesting ideas. He was a quiet young man, and no one ever suspected him of pulling pranks. The worst one he ever pulled was this:

The dean was a notorious drunk. One night, Dad and a friend watched him through the window of his house as he drank himself into a stupor and passed out. Then Dad called the local chief of police and said, "The dean of ——— College has passed."

The police went down and started to put him in a body bag—but then the dean woke up. In addition to being hungover, the dean found himself in a very bizarre and embarrassing position.

Dad and his friend had a good laugh and were never caught.

MARY, 30, NEW ROCHELLE, NEW YORK

When we were growing up, my mother was always in the kitchen or the laundry room; my dad was always out of the house, up early to jog, home late from work. At dinner, he stayed very quiet. My mother said once, "Your father doesn't know how to talk to children."

What my father knew was how to work with his hands. On the weekends, he fixed the car, built bookshelves, poured cement for a deck. My brothers stood between him and the toolbox; when he wanted something, he snapped and pointed, and one of them would scramble for a wrench or screwdriver.

On Sundays, I sat beside him in the pew at church, lifting his fingers one by one, inspecting the calluses and blisters, the dried blood beneath a fingernail that one of the boys had slammed accidentally with a hammer. I remember that when my little brother James was born, he was so small that his entire body fit inside my father's palm.

KELLY, 26, NEW YORK, NEW YORK

Just before my father was sent overseas during World War II, he and my mother resurrected an old parlor game that they would use as a code if and when they ever had to fool the ever-vigilant army censors. The code was this: The capitals of every proper name were the consonants, and the vowels were designated numerically—1 was *a*, 2 was *e*, and so on. Dad went overseas and wrote home every day, affectionate but ordinary messages.

One day, my mother was reading one of his letters and noticed that the postscript was very odd. It began with "Canfield walked four miles" and then rambled on about nothing. Mom was puzzled at first, and then with great excitement said, "I think this is in code!" When she deciphered the message, it read, "Columbus Day." She took this to mean he would be coming home Columbus Day, and, sure enough, he did!

He had been gone a year, so needless to say, we were all very, very happy!

ANN, 73, BARRINGTON, ILLINOIS

My father was a tall, stern, and rather reserved man, but every once in a while he would surprise us by showing us his softer, more sentimental side. Never was this more apparent than when there was a new moon.

From time to time, he would lead me outside the house, take me by the shoulders, and turn me to face him. "Now look over your left shoulder," he would instruct me. And so I did— to see a brand-new moon, just a sliver in the evening sky.

"It will bring you luck," he would say. And because he said it, I believed it.

I always think of him now when I see a new moon in the sky. And not long ago, when my son was going through a particularly difficult time, I took him outside one evening. "Look over your left shoulder," I said. He did, and as we looked at the new moon together, I told him about the times with my father.

BECKY, 53, OXFORD, MISSISSIPPI

In the town where I grew up, there were no chain stores, just a few family-run stores. And of all the family-run stores, none seemed to have more family than Louie's Supermarket, where I went with my dad every Saturday.

I was the third child of six, but my status as First Girl elevated me to Princess of Honor when I went to Louie's with Dad. Louie and his wife owned the store, while various siblings and in-laws ran the produce, butcher, bake shop, and other departments. Having Dad to myself was special enough, but Louie and his family treated me like a Princess Daughter of Honor as well, as we went around the store.

Louie's also sold record albums, and Dad always let me choose a new one, which we would listen to all week long. Songs by Nancy Sinatra, Herb Albert and the Tijuana Brass, and Petula Clark never fail to bring me right back to Louie's with my dad.

MEG, 44, BURLINGTON, VERMONT

My dad has never liked dogs, ever since one tried to bite him when he was a kid. He hates their smell, their germs, their drool, and the hairs and dirt they leave on his clothes.

A few years ago, our upstairs neighbor and friend had a lively German shepherd–type mutt named George. Sometimes, George would come thundering down the stairs and into our apartment (we often had our door open), his tail wagging and knocking stuff over, his claws scratching the wooden floor, and, no doubt, leaving dog hairs everywhere. (We kids loved these times.) Dad would be working at his desk and leap up, barking out orders for George to leave. As he did, George would find a way to lick Dad's knees, which would gross him out!

Then our upstairs neighbor died, which was really sad. To help his family out, and as a tribute to him, Dad ended up walking George twice a day for nearly a week. A sight I'd never thought I'd see.

NICK, 16, NEW YORK CITY, NEW YORK

❖ ❖ ❖ ❖ ❖ ❖ **148** ❖ ❖ ❖ ❖ ❖ ❖

I always admired the way my dad could dress to any environment and always look great. When we vacationed in New Mexico, Daddy could put on blue jeans, boots, and a cowboy hat and look totally natural, like a born-and-bred New Mexican. When we visited New York, Daddy would wear a Brooks Brothers straw hat and always a flower in his buttonhole. Wherever we went, he always looked outstanding.

But Daddy was most comfortable in his pajamas, just regular men's pajamas that he'd change into at home as soon as dinner was over. In fact, when he died, we all agreed that of all his outfits, he'd probably prefer to be buried in his pajamas. And so he was, with his usual dignity and elegance.

JOAN, 70, LAKE FOREST, ILLINOIS

I had recently learned to drive and had just gotten my driver's license. I was driving by myself around the town square on a rainy day. Suddenly, the car made a huge *thump!* Alarmed, I could not see what or whom I might have hit. I tried to pull over and stop, but there was no room and everyone was honking, so I just kept going.

I was very flustered when I got home because I had this horrible thought that I had hit something or done some harm. My dad assured me that it was probably a bad pothole, but he saw how upset I was and took me in his car that very minute, back to the "scene of the crime." He went the exact route I had and indeed his car did the same as mine had—it was a huge pothole.

I was relieved but also felt very good that my dad went out of his way to make sure everything, including his daughter, was okay.

ANDREA, 26, LAGUNA BEACH, CALIFORNIA

Both of my parents grew up having large, formal, after-church dinners that took up most of a Sunday afternoon, which neither could stand. Their idea of an after-church meal was: Eat whatever you want, clean up your mess, and go off to play.

In the evening, we'd have "supper" (as opposed to "dinner"). Dad would always make fish balls and popovers. Besides barbecue, this was the only meal Dad liked to make. He'd take codfish and mash it all up with a fork, then take potatoes and mash them all up and mix it all together with an egg and some seasonings. He'd roll them into balls and fry them up. Just as the fish balls were degreasing on some paper towels, he'd pull huge, fluffy popovers out of the oven and drop them into a big basket.

"Supper's ready!" he'd call. And we'd come running.

LIZA, 42, KANSAS CITY, KANSAS

I n the old days, people would get new license plates for their cars every year. My father hung every car license plate he ever owned on the wall of our garage, a veritable mosaic of metal license plates that family and friends still remember, though it's been a quarter century since Dad died.

These license plates began in 1923, with Dad's first car, and ended in 1970, when he stopped driving. Every license plate of his had the number 7843 on it, which meant he was the 7,843rd person to register for a car in the state of Massachusetts. This being a relatively low number, it conferred some status, and when Dad died, a close family relation asked to take over the number, as an heirloom of sorts.

The number 7843 lives on in our family as bank card numbers, lottery numbers, and a plain old lucky number.

PAT, 75, MACON, GEORGIA

My dad worked long, hard hours and I didn't see him very much. One way we remedied this was with a "special time" ritual: Once a week or so, we would play beauty parlor, pretending our kitchen was the famous hairdressing salon Charles of the Ritz. I would stand at the sink and my father would wash my wavy red hair. I would call him "Daddy of the Ritz."

SUZANNE, 42, IRVINGTON, NEW YORK

Every now and then, I'll see a young girl with her father and I'm reminded of myself when I was her age, and of how much I loved my dad. Once, it was the way a girl leaned her forehead on her dad's chest, maybe in frustration, and the way the father folded his hands on her back and smiled down at her; another time, at a party with mostly adults, a teenage girl leaned lightly against her father, while listening to and observing the strangers around her.

I know—at least I think I know—the quiet comfort those girls were gaining from their dads. I hope that each of them learns, as I did, that for as long as he is around, even when the girl is grown, her dad will always be there to lean on.

CAROLINE, 79, BATON ROUGE, LOUISIANA

When I was married with children, Mother and Dad came over for Sunday dinner every week. Dad would always sit at the head of the table, dishing out the meat, potatoes, and vegetables for everyone. However, Dad had no desire to give out big, heaping helpings to everyone—that, he considered wasteful. Instead, portions were small to the point of minimal. "If you want seconds, it's here," he'd say, pointing to the platters in front of him.

Dad's last name was Whiting, and the small servings of food he gave became known as—ironically among the children, but only on the six other days of the week—"a Whiting serving," as in, "Hey, you just gave me a Whiting serving of potatoes! Can't I have more?"

THEA, 69, CAMBRIDGE, MASSACHUSETTS

I call my dad Moy Moy, which means cuddle cuddle. I invented that word when I was six, because of how caring he is.

Back then, I loved our nightly routine; before tucking me into bed, he would bring me a glass of water and play a game of Candyland. As he was preparing the water, I would always cheat and put the ice-cream card second, so I could pick it when I let him go first. Years later, I realized he let me do this (the game went faster that way).

There is no way to fully describe the love that he gives—not only to me, but to everyone else he meets. He is the Moy who accepted my cuddles, who drives the seniors to church, who does the dishes, who never ever gets mad, and who cries at movies, dance recitals, and graduations.

KATIE, 20, PLANTATION, FLORIDA

My favorite movie is *Citizen Kane*. This goes back to the summer I was fourteen and totally uninterested in any movie older than I was, and especially one in black and white. But Dad rented *Citizen Kane* one week anyway because it was his favorite movie and he wanted to share it with me. I could not say no. It took us four nights to get through it, but in the end, I learned a lot about news and the news business, William Randolph Hearst and San Simeon, movies, and why well-made ones are so good (even ones you think at first you won't like).

Whenever I hear a *Citizen Kane* reference, I think of lying on the floor, a couch cushion under my head, with Dad next to me as we watched the movie. Nowadays, Dad enjoys coming to my apartment to visit and to see my cat—named Rosebud.

KATHERINE, 26, COLUMBIA, SOUTH CAROLINA

On weekends, Dad took me everywhere with him: the hardware store, the auto parts store, the tractor and farm supply store. He always held my hand as we crossed the street, even when I was old enough to be embarrassed by it. We played our favorite game holding hands.

Dad would silently squeeze my hand four times, representing the words, "Do you love me?" I'd reply with three squeezes, "Yes, I do." His answer, two squeezes, "How much?" My response was to demonstrate how much by squeezing as hard as I could, sometimes with both hands. Sometimes Dad would make me feel as though I was very strong and other times he would tease me with a hurt look and say, "Gee, you must not love me very much." This always brought on another, more demonstrative squeeze. There's still not enough strength in my hands to show how much I love him.

CLAIRE, 38, TUCSON, ARIZONA

I remember when Dad used to take my little sister, Kelli, and me every Sunday to play miniature golf. Dad would always let us pick the color ball we wanted and take the leftover color as his own. To this day, Kelli and I still fight over who gets to go first and what color ball we want, and my Dad still always goes last and always wins.

TRACEE, 27, LANCASTER, PENNSYLVANIA

As a boy growing up, I was always curious about my father's experiences during World War II. Was Dad shot at? Had he been afraid? Was he a hero?

Occasionally, Dad would tell me a story, like the time kamikaze pilots had almost hit the ship that he was on. "Did you shoot at them? Did you kill them?" I asked. But he never answered.

Years later, just before his death, my father, my wife, and I were watching a TV special on WWII veterans, and I asked my father, one more time, "Did you ever shoot any Japanese soldiers?" And with my back to him, I heard him say no, but my wife later told me that he had been nodding his head yes.

I guess even though you grow to be a man, there are still things your father wants to protect you from. And I realize now that fighting a war isn't what makes your dad a hero. He's a hero because he is your dad.

ROGER, 54, LAKE WORTH, FLORIDA